PECKHAM PATTER

PECKHAM PATTER

THE COMPLETE WIT AND WISDOM OF

ONLY FOOLS *and* ★★★ HORSES

DAN SULLIVAN
From the scripts by John Sullivan OBE

Ebury Spotlight, an imprint of Ebury Publishing
20 Vauxhall Bridge Road, London SW1V 2SA

Ebury Spotlight is part of the Penguin Random House group of companies
whose addresses can be found at global.penguinrandomhouse.com

Penguin
Random House
UK

Consultant: Jim Sullivan | Consultant Editor: Steve Clark

By arrangement with Splendid Books Limited. Previously published as
The Wit and Wisdom of Only Fools & Horses and *More Wit & Wisdom
of Only Fools & Horses*

First published by Ebury Spotlight in 2021
Photographs: Radio Times (except page 7 ITV/Shutterstock)

www.penguin.co.uk

A CIP catalogue record for this book is available from the British Library

ISBN 9781529148794

Printed and bound in Great Britain by Clays Ltd, Elcograf S.p.A.

Imported into the EEA by Penguin Random House Ireland, Morrison Chambers,
32 Nassau Street, Dublin D02 YH68.

Penguin Random House is committed to a sustainable future for our business,
our readers and our planet. This book is made from Forest Stewardship
Council® certified paper.

MIX
Paper from
responsible sources
FSC FSC® C018179

TABLE OF CONTENTS

FOREWORD

by SIR DAVID JASON OBE

To pay homage to the wit and wisdom of the brilliant dialogue and comic lines in Only Fools and Horses is really a massive tribute to the writer and my dear friend, John Sullivan.

John created the series, wrote the series and nurtured the characters into the ones we all know and continue to know now. With John's untimely death in 2011, I am more than happy to applaud his comic genius and talents through this very funny and insightful book as I consider it a privilege to have been a part of such a wonderful team.

I say a team, as it really was an amazing group of people who worked on Only Fools from the cast, to the production team right through the ranks. It really didn't feel right being paid to have so much fun and very often we were in hysterics for a large part of the day, which didn't always go down too well with the Director and Producer.

One moment in particular was the Batman and Robin sequence. Every time I looked at Rodney (Nicky Lyndhurst) dressed as Robin I just fell about laughing, and of course every time he looked at me dressed as Batman with my silly little bat ears he was equally convulsed.

As I once acknowledged at a BAFTA evening, John gave me the ammunition and I fired the gun and I know the rest of the cast felt that too. John had a great talent in keeping his finger on the nation's pulse and his humour was very much on trend at the time of writing. He took into account the political and social climate and weaved that into the Only Fools' story lines, so he really did often speak for a large majority of the nation with respect to the fashion and struggles of its day. His language was street language and he reflected a culture which showed humour and pathos in equal measure. We are all aware of the wit of John Sullivan but his exquisite observations of ordinary life show the wisdom in spadefuls. For that and the fun we had and the history we made – I just have to say a big and heartfelt Cushty!

Sir David Jason OBE – aka Del Boy

ARTS, MUSIC & LITERATURE

'As Macbeth said to Hamlet in Midsummer Night's Dream, "we've been done up like a couple of kippers"'

DEL

'I'm a Ming fan myself. He made some wonderful stuff, that Ming. Pity he went and died when he did'

DEL

'I saw your face when that Adrian asked me what I thought about Hamlet and I said I preferred Castella'

DEL TO RAQUEL

'Del used to be cultural advisor to the Chelsea shed'

RODNEY

'It's a funny thing, your Lordship, but van Coff happens to be my favourite artist 'un all'

DEL

VICKY: 'I was at the Milan School of Art for two years, then I had a spell at the Sorbonne. Where were you?'
RODNEY: 'Basingstoke'

'It's not supposed to get going, it's culture. You don't come to an opera to enjoy it, you come 'cause... it's there'

DEL ON OPERA

'You could make the Elgin marbles sound like a second-hand Datsun'

RODNEY TO DEL

'Once you've seen one Rubens,
you've seen 'em all'

DEL

RAQUEL: 'I don't know about you but I just
love the works of Shaw'
DEL: 'Oh yeah... "like a puppet on a string..."'

'One day they might make a musical
about the history of the Trotter family.
Then as a sequel they could do
Schindler's List On Ice'

RODNEY

DEL: 'What about that poster you showed us, when you was top of the bill with Otis Redding at the Talk of the Town, London?'
RAQUEL: 'It was Laurie London at the Talk of the Town, Reading'

'You didn't honestly believe all that rubbish, did yer? That you and them wallies were destined for the Albert Hall, the Carnegie Hall? The only "hall" you lot was destined for was "sod all"'

DEL TO RODNEY

'Putting me in a pair of green wellies will not turn me into Archduke Ferdinand. I will be Rodney Trotter in a pair of green wellies'

RODNEY

'The only times my clothes look fashionable is when I'm watching UK Gold'

RAQUEL

'You stick me in front of the telly with a Singapore Sling, a ham sandwich and a bit of Chekhov and I'm as happy as a sand boy'

DEL

DEL ON MIRANDA: *'She's very impressed. She knows I know a lot about antiques, don't she?'*
RODNEY: *'Oh yeah. Well, you've been out with a few, ain't yer?'*

'I heard that she was the one that cut the ribbon on the opening of Stonehenge'

DEL ON ELSIE PARTRIDGE

'We gave you the world's greatest sailors, pal.
Remember that. We gave you Nelson, we gave you
Drake, we gave you Columbus'

DEL TO AN AMERICAN

'Del, you can't speak French. You're still struggling
with English'

RODNEY

'How can I change the lywics to "Cwying"?
The bloody song's called "Cwying"!'

TONY ANGELINO

*'He made one great film and then you
never saw him again'*

TRIGGER ON GANDHI

MIRANDA: *'Do you like Cezanne?'*
DEL: *'Oh yeah; a bit of ice and lemonade,
it's lovely'*

HISTORY

'The way those Germans were carrying on, someone was gonna get hurt '

GRANDAD ON WWII

'Everyone's entitled to a cup of tea, Rodney. I mean, it's in the Magna Carta or something'

GRANDAD

'I'm a great fan of the Byzantine period, myself. I don't think you can whack 'em'

DEL

'Cold? You bits of kids don't know the meaning of the word. You should've been with me on the Russian convoys. One night it was so cold, the flame on my lighter froze'

ALBERT

'While the nation celebrated, they were hidden away in big grey buildings far from the public gaze. I mean, courage like that could put you right off your victory dinner, couldn't it? They promised us homes fit for heroes. They give us heroes fit for homes'

GRANDAD ON THE
SOLDIERS RETURNING FROM WWI

'All the dreaming and the scheming and the chasing and the trying, that was the fun part, y'know. It was like... it was dangerous, it was impossible. It was like Columbo sailing away to find America'

DEL

'... one day we were attacked by a Kamikaze pilot. He came zooming in towards us – I remember saying to the skipper, "the way he's carrying on he'll kill himself"'

ALBERT

'That's a bit of history you're holding there, and I mean real history. Not like them Nelson's eye patches Del Boy used to flog to the tourists'

GRANDAD

BUSINESS

'I'm out there on the yuppy tightrope, me. Nerves on red alert, a beta blocker and a dream, that's me. I eat on the move, a mobile phone in one hand and a pot noodle in the other'

DEL

'Mine is not to reason why, mine is but to sell and buy'

DEL

'A conscience is nice, but business is business'

DEL

'They're yuppies. They don't speak proper
English like what we do'

DEL

'My motto is "West End goods at Southend prices"'

DEL

'Del thinks all you need is a Filofax and a pair of red
braces and you're chairman of the board'

RODNEY

'I'm afraid the company's finished, it's gone. Trotters Independent Traders is no more. It's kaput, it's dead, dead as the emu'

DEL

'Asking a Trotter if he knows anything about chandeliers is like asking Mr Kipling if he knows anything about cakes'

DEL

'We are doing well, relatively speaking. I mean, we are doing well compared to an Iranian gin salesman'

DEL

'Oh well, you win some, you lose some. Nothing ventured, nothing gained. It's, well, boeuf a la mode, as the French say'

DEL

'He wants me to stand in a market, flogging raincoats with "dry clean only" on the label'

RODNEY ON DEL

RODNEY: 'They could have you under the Trades Descriptions Act. You call it Peckham Spring but it ain't from a spring'

DEL: 'Yeah, well Sainsbury's, they sell runner beans but they ain't been round the track three times, have they?'

'Modern business people only speak in initials,
don't they? You know, you've got
FT – Financial Times, BA – British Airways,
GLC – General 'Lectric Company'

DEL

'You see, Dave, a losing streak is like joining the
Moonies. Easy to get into but a bark to get out of'

TRIGGER TO RODNEY

'You need specialised equipment for a job like this. Refined glass brushes, advanced soldering gear. What are we gonna use, eh? Super glue and a bottle of Windolene, knowing you'

RODNEY ON CHANDELIER CLEANING

'Well, that is it Miranda. I have discussed the matter with my partner and we both agree that we shall exceed to your delusions'

DEL

'When Corrine comes back in here she's gonna find her kettle's been knackered, her kitchen's been turned into a Turkish bath and she's got a Kentucky fried canary at the bottom of a cage... and we're gonna say "paint fumes did it!"'

DEL

'It's amazing, innit? Everything you buy off him's got something missing'

BOYCIE ON DEL

'You see, Abdul's cousin's girlfriend's brother's mate's mate, right, he's a gamekeeper down at one of them private zoos and Monkey Harris' sister's husband's first wife's stepfather, right, works for an animal food company, so put the two together, what you got? A nice little earner'

DEL

'Del, thanks to your high profile, we now have a company called "TIT" and a director with "DIC" after his name'

RODNEY

'They stopped making spares for that van years ago. I've tried everywhere. Breakers' yards, spares shops, archaeologists...'

RODNEY

'Del, these dolls ain't called Barbie or Cindy. These dolls are called Lusty Linda and Erotic Estelle'

RODNEY

'He's the sort of bloke, if he had a flower shop, right, he'd close on St Valentine's Day'

DEL ON RODNEY

'As it happens, I know this little bloke down in Wapping, he'll fix you up a treat. He's Iranian but he has contacts in Persia'

DEL

'Now, all this equipment here, is manufactured by the one country that leads the world in Alpine clothing, namely Fiji'

DEL

'These canteens of cutlery are a very exclusive line. You can only buy these at Harrods, Liberty's and Patel's Multimart'

DEL

'With your diploma and my yuppy image, we're on the way up'

DEL TO RODNEY

'Look, I spend half my life trying to hide my business deals. The last thing I need is to have 'em all recorded on a floppy bloody disc'

MIKE

'This is sonic, state-of-the-art technology, this. And this is none of your Japanese or your German rubbish, no sir, this is actually made in Albania'

DEL

'Enjoy ourselves? Del, we are two thousand pounds in debt, we have a garage load of hooky doors and a mob of irate Rastafarians after our blood'

RODNEY

'I mean, if some weirdo wants to get it going with half a pound of latex and a lump of oxygen, that's his business. As far as I'm concerned, he could have a meaningful relationship with a barrage balloon'

DEL

'Menage a trois! In the middle of the worst winter for two million years, with the weather man laying odds on a new Ice Age, this dipstick goes and buys out Ambre Solaire'

DEL ON RODNEY

'He helps me and I help him. It's "conseil d'etat" as they say in Grenobles'

DEL

'I've got an early call in the morning. I've gotta get down to Peckham by seven to pick up a consignment of fire-damaged woks'

DEL

FAMILY

'There was Mum, bless her. I mean, she tried but her health let her down. Then there was Dad; he would've loved a job except he suffered from this sticky mattress. And there was dear old Grandad, bless him. He was about as useful as a pair of sunglasses on a bloke with one ear'

DEL

'Rodney's got some very nice qualities. I mean, she might've been smitten by his rakish charms or his boyish good looks. On the other hand she could be a posh tart fancying a bit of scrag'

DEL

'Look at the way you dress to begin with. You make a Christmas tree look sombre'

RODNEY TO DEL

'I wear a trendy trench coat and Gordon Gecko braces. You wear a lumberjack's coat and Gordon Bennett boots'

DEL TO RODNEY

'Your dad always said that one day, Del would reach the top. There again, he used to say that one day Millwall would win the cup'

GRANDAD

'I've lived with him for all these years and I thought I really knew him and then something like this happens, some simple gesture and then you suddenly realise what a 100 per cent, 24-carat plonker he really is'

DEL ON RODNEY

'What about the time he was in the navy, eh? Every single ship he ever sailed on either got torpedoed or dive-bombed... two of 'em in peacetime'

RODNEY ON ALBERT

'Freddie the Frog... killed himself by sitting on someone else's detonator... what a plonker'

RODNEY

'D'you remember your cousin Audrey? I went to stay with her and her husband, Kevin, for a year. One day, he sent me down to Sainsbury's with a shopping list. When I came back, they'd emigrated'

ALBERT

'God knows how you've got the courage to walk down dark alleys wearing all that gold. When they see you coming you must look like a mugger's pension scheme'

RODNEY TO DEL

'I've heard rumours Mickey Mouse wears a Rodney Trotter wristwatch'

BOYCIE

'While all the other Mods were having punch ups down at Southend and going to The Who concerts, I was at home babysitting. I could never get your oyster milk stains out of my Ben Sherman's. I used to find rusks in me Hush Puppies'

DEL

'You know what his last job was, don't yer? He was entertainments officer on the Belgrano'

DEL ON ALBERT

'Let's face it, Del, most of your French phrases come straight out of a Citroen manual'

RODNEY

DEL: *'The French have a word for people like me'*
RODNEY: *'Yeah, the English have got a couple of good 'uns, un all'*

'It was nothing to do with me, Del. I only suggested it'

GRANDAD

'Of course you wouldn't remember me. Not at my mum's wedding. I was only a babe in arms'

DEL

'Do you remember Rodney? He used to be a little scruff. Look at him now... he's a big scruff'

DEL

'It wasn't me, Del Boy, it was me brain'

GRANDAD

'I'd have to get done for chicken molesting to bring a slur on this family's name'

RODNEY

'He sold his soul for an ounce of Old Holborn years ago'

DEL ON HIS DAD

'He died a couple of years before I was born'

TRIGGER ON HIS DAD

'He was an out of work lamp lighter waiting for gas to make a comeback'

DEL ON GRANDAD

'There's a moral to this story, Del Boy, but for the life of me, I can't find it'

GRANDAD

'I can almost see my grandad now. Sitting by the fire, one leg on the fender, other one in the corner'

TRIGGER ON HIS ONE-LEGGED GRANDAD

'I used to miss my dad, until I learnt to punch straight'

DEL

'*You look like a blood donor who couldn't say no*'

DEL TO RODNEY

'*Raquel's got post-natal depression, Albert's got post-naval depression and Damien keeps chucking toys at my head*'

RODNEY

'*That is England's greatest little sailor since Nelson lost the Armada*'

DEL ON ALBERT

'D'you realise, by the time I'm 45, son of Del will be 16 and that'll be it, I can hear it now. "I've got a good idea, Uncle Rodney. I'll go and buy a load of old crap and you can go out and sell it for me"'

RODNEY

'I'm talking about men and women. You, you're still knocking around with Brownies'

DEL TO RODNEY

'You mean to say that somebody actually trusted you with their property? That's like trusting a Piranha fish with your finger... or worse'

DEL TO GRANDAD

'Us being such a law-abiding family, we don't really know how to converse with the Old Bill'

DEL

'He tried to join the police force once. It was after he failed the intelligence test to become a Unigate milkman'

DEL ON RODNEY

'We were just two lonely people. Arthur was away in the army and your gran had just departed... oh no, she hadn't died, just departed'

GRANDAD

'You must've spent a third of your life standing in front of mirrors. My earliest childhood recollection is of you standing in front of a mirror. Up until I was four, I thought you was twins'

RODNEY TO DEL

'What are you gonna stitch Grandad up with, eh? Found in possession of a forged bus pass? Demanding protection money from the local Darby & Joan club?'

DEL TO SLATER

RODNEY: *'Why did you tell me I'd go away for ten years as a special category prisoner, that they'd nicknamed me the Peckham Pouncer, that there was gangs of men roaming the streets, looking to hang me from the nearest lamp post?'*
DEL: *'For a laugh'*

'Grandad! It's Christmas night and I am stuck in here with y... I'm stuck in here, watching a film the Germans tried to bomb'

RODNEY

'Don't be fooled by him, Rodney. He's had everything from Galloping Lurgy to Saturday Night Fever'

DEL ON HIS DAD

RODNEY: 'Are you trying to tell me that my dad was in a band?'
DEL: 'No Rodney, no. Just the brass section'

'Well, I can't wait to fill in my next passport application form... Mother's name: Joan Mavis Trotter, Father's name: Herb Alpert and the Tijuana Brass'

RODNEY

'They found out they didn't have a patient called Trotter, but they did have a porter called Trotter... but he left two weeks ago with 57 blankets, 133 pairs of rubber gloves and the chief gynaecologist's Lambretta'

DEL ON HIS DAD

'He was a trainee chef at the Ear, Nose and Throat Hospital'

DEL ON GRANDAD

'Take no notice of him. He's an old sailor. He's still got a bit of depth charge lodged in his brain'

DEL ON ALBERT

'The last time he had his leg over, Nelson
Mandela was in borstal'

DEL ON ALBERT

'You dozy little twonk, Rodney. You bang on the
roof of my van again like that, it won't be "Frankie
goes to Hollywood", it'll be "Rodney goes
to Hospital"'

DEL

'Whatever the subject is, Mum had something to
say about it on her deathbed. She must've spent
her final few hours in this mortal realm doing
nothing but rabbiting'

RODNEY

'You take that time you was done for the possession of cannabis. I came here and I told Mum that her little baby was in trouble with the law and it was almost as if I could hear her voice saying to me "bribe the Old Bill, Del"'

DEL TO RODNEY

'Mum will be there 'cause she'll be wanting to see Rodney, her little wonder baby. She always used to call him that you know, 'cause she wondered how the hell he happened'

DEL ON HEAVEN

'Our mum was a wonderful woman. She had long golden, blonde hair... sometimes'

DEL TO RODNEY

'It's a good thing your mum died when she did 'cause that would've killed her'

GRANDAD TO DEL

'Me and your Aunt Ada didn't talk to each other for years but she was still my wife'

ALBERT

'I do remember... sort of, but it's misty... This blonde lady and... she was there and then she wasn't. Bit like the SDP really'

RODNEY ON HIS MUM

'I don't believe this conversation. In 35 seconds, you two have married me, buried me and given me widow skin trouble'

RODNEY

TRIGGER: 'Did you ever meet my nan?'
RODNEY: 'Well, only at her funeral'

'That bloke has been in shark-infested seas, he's been attacked by Kamikaze pilots and blown up more times than a beach ball'

DEL ON ALBERT

'If that Freddie the Frog was going out with a married woman on this estate, why did he leave all his money to our mum?'

DEL

'She knew who my dad was... roughly'

TRIGGER ON HIS MUM

'He may be perverted but he's not dangerous'

DEL ON RODNEY

ALBERT: **'When I came to live with you two,
I hoped that I'd end my days here'**
RODNEY: **'Yeah, so did we'**

ALBERT: **'D'you know what'd look good on you,
Rodney? A big white Stetson'**
RODNEY: **'D'you know what'd look good on you,
Albert? A Dobermann pinscher!'**

61

RODNEY: *'Well, if I've always been such a let-down, why did you insist on having me around?'*
DEL: *'To keep my promise to Mum... and you never know when you might need some bone marrow'*

'I do not believe what that garrity old git has done to us. I mean, the only hole he hasn't fallen down is the black one in Calcutta'

DEL ON ALBERT

'My mum was a lady. D'you know, she was the first woman in Peckham to smoke menthol cigarettes?'

DEL

'Del's gotta be the only bloke who can buy a gold identity bracelet and take it to a dyslexic engraver'

RODNEY

GRANDAD ON MICKEY PEARCE: 'He'd rob his own grandmother, he would'
RODNEY: 'Oh, don't be stupid Grandad...
that was never proved'

'Stone me, Rodney! We see more of Hayley's Comet than we do of him'

DEL ON HIS DAD

'Look, understand one thing Cass, I am not getting like Del. No way Pedro!'

RODNEY

'Last week, we was having a row about whose turn it was to go down the chippy and you claimed that Mum said, on her deathbed, "send Rodney for the fish"'

RODNEY TO DEL

*'They reckon when he boarded his last ship,
the crew shot an Albatross for luck'*

RODNEY ON ALBERT

GRANDAD: **'Del Boy, I'd like to be cremated'**
DEL: **'Well, you'll have to wait 'til the morning,
'cause they'll be closed now'**

SLATER: **'Is this your grandad?'**
DEL: **'No, that's the au pair, innit?'**

'You should come round to Trotter Towers with me one morning, Cass. It'd give Terry Waite the shakes. You can't move for teething rings, Farley's rusks and funny smells. It's like Nightmare on Sesame Street'

RODNEY

ALBERT: *'Del wouldn't mind if I borrowed some of his after shave, would he?'*
RODNEY: *'What d'you wanna use after shave for? You've got Epping bloody Forest growing out of your chin'*

'It's like my dear old mum used to say "There's none so blind as them what won't listen"'

DEL

'When you get to twenty and your six-year-old brother is taller than you are, it makes you think, dunnit?'

DEL

'You're not interested, Rodney, are yer? So it's purely epidemic innit, eh?'

DEL

'I've already been through the Adriatic with him once this afternoon. It's like the adventures of a Dover sole'

RODNEY ON ALBERT

'He used to go to work on a horse. And even then he got the sack after two days for wallpapering over a serving hatch'

RODNEY ON GRANDAD

'Rodney, why don't you go in the kitchen and put your head in the food blender?'

DEL

FOOD & DRINK

'I've had a lot of sobering thoughts in my time, Del Boy. It were them that started me drinking'

GRANDAD

'What kind of financial advisor goes out to buy an emperor burger and comes back with a cheese burger?'

GRANDAD

'If you had been in charge of the Last Supper it would've been a take away'

RODNEY TO DEL

'She had a bit of aggro with the chicken tikka. Mind you, it was a bit rubbery. She was chewing on one bit for about half an hour. I thought she'd end up blowing bubbles with it'

DEL

'All I asked you to do was put the box of wine in the fridge and me tub of Neapolitan ice cream in the freezer, but no, you get that arse about face, don't yer? So come nine o'clock all I could offer her was a bowl of gunge and a Beaujolais ice lolly'

DEL TO GRANDAD

'No, no Rodney. I'll get the sandwiches 'cause you bought the Rolls'

DEL

'Seems like nothing's gonna change my luck. Raquel says we ought to try Feng Shui. I said to her "what good is eating raw fish gonna do?"'

DEL

'Come on, let's go down to Sid's cafe. Whenever we reach historic moments like this, I feel like a fry up'

DEL

'If a nightingale sang, now, in Berkeley Square, someone would eat it'

DEL

'Michael, Michael! Please, a bottle of Champagne
for my partner and me... and make it the best
Champagne, a bottle of that Dillinger's '75'

DEL

DEL: 'One of my most favouritest meals
is duck a l'orange, but I don't know how
to say that in French'
RODNEY: 'It's canard'
DEL: 'You can say that again bruv'

'That curry's doing a conga in my colon'

BOYCIE, ON HAVING EATEN DEL'S
HOMEMADE 'CHICKEN TROTTER' CURRY

'Pint of lager, Rodney. They'd sold right
out of Pina Coladas, Del, so I got you a
Mackeson instead'

GRANDAD

'Pork scratchings? Sounds like a pig with fleas'

DEL

'I'm a caviar person, me, you know... most probably'

DEL

'Food is for wimps'

DEL

FRIENDSHIP

RODNEY: *'I'm just seeing my mates, that's all'*
DEL: *'Yeah but why are they always the same mates, eh? Johnnie Walker and Ron Bacardi?'*

'When Boycie was born, the midwife held him up and slapped his mother'

DEL

'Ere Boyce. You know this car's a GTI. If you rearrange the letters, you've got yourself a personalised number plate'

DEL

RODNEY: *'Del, why do they call him Trigger?*
Does he carry a gun?'
DEL: *'No, it's 'cause he looks like a horse'*

'Have you ever spent an evening in Trigger's flat?
It's like having a séance with Mr Bean'

BOYCIE

'And who are your mates, Del? Boycie, the
freemason, a total snob who thinks anyone who's
got a pound less than him is a peasant, Denzil
is a man who eats porridge with a wig in it, and
then there's Trigger, a road sweeper who gives pet
names to his teeth'

RODNEY

'Trigger? With a computer? Do me a favour, he's still struggling with light switches'

RODNEY

'Come on Del, there's gotta be something behind this 'cause Boycie would scalp you if dandruff had a going rate'

RODNEY

'You've got to be very careful. I mean, Trig gets very emotional. He's Italian on his dad's friend's side'

DEL

'He's the sort of bloke what buys a tin of baked beans on Tuesday so he can have a bubble bath on Wednesday'

DEL ON BOYCIE

'Trigger, you haven't got a family history. You were created by a chemical spillage at a germ warfare factory somewhere off the Deptford High Street'

BOYCIE

'I can't understand it, Del. I mean, all you've ever done is ruin his wedding reception, almost break up his marriage, flood his kitchen and steal his two-thousand-pound redundancy money and he goes and gets all silly about it'

RODNEY ON DENZIL

'Mickey Pearce? He couldn't keep a rabbit going with lettuce'

DEL

'Parcels attract attention these days. Best to carry it openly, then it don't look conspicious'

TRIGGER

'You know what happened to the real Trigger, don't yer? Roy Rogers had him stuffed'

DEL

'What's the name of that bloke who invented the Dyson vacuum cleaner?'

TRIGGER

'Give my love to Marlene... everyone else used to'

SLATER TO BOYCIE

'He ain't got a few grasses, he's got an entire lawn'

DEL ON SLATER

'According to you and your family, we are looking for a six-foot-seven-inch dwarf, aged between 15 and 50. A white male with Oriental features who's as black as Newgate's knocker... oh yeah, he wears a deaf aid'

SLATER

'Oh by the way, if you come across Denzil, tell him I tried to phone him twice last night but I haven't got his number'

BRENDAN TO DEL

'Albie Littlewood, my bestest friend in all the world. The greatest pal a bloke could have... and all the time he was doinking my bird'

DEL

'For God's sake, Marlene. I might be able to con people into buying my cars, I might be able to convince 'em that you conceived and gave birth in seven days flat, but how the hell am I gonna persuade 'em my Grandad was Louis Armstrong?!!!'

BOYCIE

'An hour ago, you was "The Shadow", right, a man of mystery. Now we know your name, your address and your mum's shoe size'

DEL TO LENNOX GILBEY

'I am gonna see if I can buy myself a little doll that looks something like you and then I'm going to burn it'

BOYCIE TO DEL

'What? Tell Boycie a sob story? You've gotta be joking. He's the one that cheered when Bambi's mum died'

DEL

CORRINE ON DEL: 'Denzil, how can you trust this man? Every time you meet him you end up drunk or out of pocket'
DENZIL: 'Yeah I know, but he's a mate'

'The only time you ever made women jealous was the night you won the last house at bingo'

DEL TO MICKEY PEARCE

'That bloke's been on the dole for so long, they invite him to the staff dance'

DEL ON MICKEY PEARCE

'Come on Roy, you didn't lose your friends... you didn't have any to lose in the first place'

DEL TO SLATER

'He's everywhere I go, you know. He's on the phone to me, he's at my front door, he's in the betting shop, he's in the pub and now he's in the bloody traffic jam. You know what, Rodney, I get this feeling he's haunting me, know what I mean?'

DENZIL ON DEL

*'Well, this has been nice, like old school days.
You and me sat at the same desk... only this time
you didn't put frog spawn in my milk'*

SLATER TO DEL

TRIGGER: *'When we was at school Del was the best
in our class at chemistry. He used to sell homemade
fireworks. He even blew up the science lab once'*
DENZIL: *'Yes, I remember. I was doing detention in
there at the time'*

ALBERT: *'Rodney, innit?'*
RODNEY: *'Well, it is when Trigger ain't about, yeah'*

DENZIL: *'For all we know he could be part of Al-Qaeda!'*
DEL: *'Does he look like he works in a furniture store?'*

RELIGION

DEL: *'I have come to confess my sins'*
PRIEST: *'Del, please. I've been invited out to dinner this evening'*

'There's cardinals and archbishops, they've been in the business all their lives; they never got a sniff of a miracle. Then along comes Del; he's in the game five minutes and already he's a prophet'

RODNEY

'Trigger couldn't organise a prayer in a mosque'

BOYCIE

'Something happened to me, Rodney. It came like a blinding flash of light. It was like St Paul's journey on the road to... Tobascus'

DEL

'I apologise for him, sir. It's his religion. He's an Orthodox tight arse'

DEL ON MIKE

'Christmas is a religious festival. It's meant to be boring'

DEL

SLATER: 'Whilst in prison, I found Jesus!'
DEL: 'What had they fitted him up with?'

'"It looked alright from the outside!" That's what
the Christians said about the Coliseum'

DEL

'Listen to me. With the money you could earn
out of this, you could have that place repaired,
redecorated and get Samantha Fox to re-open it
for yer'

DEL TO PRIEST

HEALTH

RODNEY: *'Bloody hell, I'm going bald!'*
ALBERT: *'It might not be that, Rodney. You might have a touch of Alopecia'*

'Once when I was a kid, I was doing my homework and I asked him what a cubic foot was. He said he didn't know but he'd tried to have a week off work with it'

DEL ON HIS DAD

'Haemorrhoids? They were more like asteroids. The surgeon said it was keyhole surgery... he forgot to say it was the keyhole to the Tower of soddin' London'

DENZIL

'I'm only concerned with Grandad. Look at him, his brain went years ago, now his legs have gone. It's only the middle bit of him left'

DEL

'The doctor reckons that I've got more tadpoles than they've got in the Serpentine'

DEL

'I don't know why they want these drug addiction centres, anyhow. I mean, ain't we got enough drug addicts without them recruiting them?'

GRANDAD

'Look, Rodney's brought you some oranges.
I'll put 'em over there, shall I, with the other
three thousand?'

DEL TO GRANDAD

'You wanna be a bit more careful about your
health, son. In the last half hour you've done so
much boot licking, you could be coming down with
cherry blossom poisoning'

GRANDAD TO SLATER

'There was this woman. She weren't feeling very
well. I don't know what was wrong with her but
she stunk of booze'

RODNEY

'You'd make an albino look bronzed'

DEL TO RODNEY

*'Oh listen to me, hospitals do not send home para-
lysed people by bus... What was it you were after,
Del, eh? Sympathy from Lisa or a disabled sticker
for the van?'*

RODNEY

'He's been firing more blanks than the territorials'

MARLENE ON BOYCIE

'Ten years from now, I won't be able to raise a smile, let alone anything else'

DEL

'D'you realise, if all my veins and arteries were stretched out in a line, they'd circle the world twice?'

ALBERT

RODNEY: 'She's most probably at the right temperature'
DEL: 'Stone me, Rodney! What are you two trying for, a baby or a barbecue?'

MISS MCKENZIE: *'Actually, when I left school,
I wanted to be a choreographer'*
DEL: *'Did you really? What a coincidence,
'cause I always wanted to go into the medical
profession myself'*

*'A year ago, you and Cassandra were really trying
for this baby, weren't ya? I mean, you was at it like
a pair of goats. I remember that you became so
pale, you had to have your passport photo redone'*

DEL TO RODNEY

*'I remember the night that Damien was born.
It was a wonderful, wonderful moment. But it was
very, very traumatic and very, very stressful.
But it wasn't a walk in the park for you, Raquel,
was it, either?'*

DEL

*'I know you don't want to have an operation.
Nobody wants to have an operation but
everyone, at some time in their lives, has
to have one and today it's your turn'*

DEL TO ALBERT

*'It sort of burnt me right across the forehead here.
The bloke who sold it to me said it was a hairdryer.
It turns out to be an electric paint stripper'*

MIKE TO A DOCTOR IN A & E

*'It's a right blinding Christmas this has turned out
to be, innit? I mean, some people get wise men,
bearing gifts. We get a wally with a disease'*

DEL

LIFE

'I've got this horrible feeling that if there is such a thing as reincarnation, knowing my luck, I'll come back as me'

RODNEY

'He who sticks his nose into a beehive will get more than a nostrilful of honey!'

DEL

'There's nothing worse than Weetabix in a beard, is there?'

RODNEY

'We have an old saying that's been handed down by generations of road sweepers. "Look after your broom"'

TRIGGER

'I've always been an achiever... I never actually achieved nothing, mind you, but I've always been in with a shout'

DEL

'He who dares wins, he who hesitates... don't'

DEL

'You should never light a candle when you've got a man with a beard in the house'

ALBERT

'Trigger doesn't have many friends or opportunity for social outlet. Every weekend he goes to the park and throws bread to the ducks. To him it's a dinner party'

BOYCIE

'Squirrels ain't got computers but they know where their nuts are'

DEL

'I feel like a turkey that's just caught Bernard Matthews grinning at him'

DEL

'I've survived all my life with a smile and a prayer. I'm Del Boy, "good old Del Boy. He's got more bounce than Zebedee"'

DEL

'Everyone's a winner, petit dejeuner'

DEL

'Please don't give up. Remember what Churchill
said, he said "Up the Alamo!"'

DEL

'The French have a saying, Rodney. "Bouillabaisse
mon ami"'

DEL

GIRL: 'What do you prefer, Rodney?
Astroturf or grass?'
RODNEY: 'I don't know, I've never smoked
Astroturf'

'I dunno what the younger generation's coming to. They can't even swear without effin' and blindin''

DEL

'What a life, eh? Me wife don't love me, me mum's left me and some bastard's nicked me bike'

RODNEY

'There are people on death row with more motivation than me'

RODNEY

'My image says "I'm going to the top, flat out."
Your image says "I'm going back to bed 'cause
I'm shagged out"'

DEL TO RODNEY

'Running away only wears out your shoes'

DEL

'I'm on top of the world. I feel like a
born-again eunuch'

RODNEY

'I am 24 years old, I have two GCEs, 13 years of schooling and three terms at an adult education centre behind me and with all that, what have I become?... I'm a lookout'

RODNEY

'You can't trust the Old Bill, can yer? Look at that time they planted six gas cookers in my bedroom'

DEL

'It's only E-type Jaguars and Sebastian Coe that make me feel proud to be British these days'

BOYCIE

'That is the mentality of your spoon-fed student type. They walk around all day with "Steve Bilko" written on their T-shirts, spouting about humanity. When it comes to a fight over a torn fiver, they make Genghis Khan look like a pacifist'

DEL

'A right blinding night I've had. I've become a member of a gay club, discovered my brother's a pervo and had a close encounter with two dockers in drag'

DEL

'I can now leap out of a Vauxhall Velox "Dukes of Hazzard" fashion, make a chapatti and say "get stuffed" in Urdu'

RODNEY

'It's better to know you've lost than not to know you've won'

JOAN TROTTER

'I'm one of them that's accepted anywhere. Whether it's drinking lager with the market boys down at Nine Elms or sipping Pimm's fruit cup at Hendon Regatta'

DEL

'It's an apartment in a complex... a tall complex. Very sophisticated actually. It's got... lifts and everything'

RODNEY ON THE FLAT

'We live half a mile up in the sky in this Lego set, built by the council'

DEL ON THE FLAT

'We run a three-wheel van with a bald tyre. We drink in wine bars where the only thing that's got a vintage is the governor's wife'

DEL

RODNEY: 'I saw a movement in the trees'
DEL: 'Of course you saw a movement in the trees. There's a ruddy typhoid blowing out there'

'Would any self-respecting axe murderer pop upstairs for 40 winks and leave his chopper in the sideboard?'

DEL

'Del, desperate men on the run don't pop home to borrow a tin opener'

RODNEY

'I remember me and Albie Littlewood. We let a couple of tyres down once. You should've seen the palaver it caused. Everyone had to get off the bus'

DEL

'It's easily done, constable. You're walking along the street, your mind on other things. You take your handkerchief out your pocket and BANG! your microwave falls on the ground'

SLATER

'Not only have you managed to sink every aircraft carrier and battleship that you've ever sailed on, but now you've gone and knackered a gravy boat'

DEL TO ALBERT

RODNEY: *'Wherever I lay my hat, that's my home. That's the sort of guy I am'*
TRIGGER: *'Yeah? You got a hat then now have you, Dave?'*

'It'll all be "Rez de Chaussee" as they say in the Doudogne'

DEL

'Women are from Venus, men are from Peckham'

RAQUEL

'"Après moi la deluge" as they say in the Latin Quarter'

DEL

RODNEY: *'I'd heard that because of the precarious state of the world, Boycie and Marlene had decided against starting a family'*
VICAR: *'Oh really? I'd heard Boycie was a Jaffa'*

'Everything's alright Rodney. I mean, we've got no money, no business and our future's about as bright as a Yugoslavian tour operator's, but no, everything's cushty!'

DEL

'"I'll be back". He always says that. D'you know what his nickname is? The Turbanator'

DEL ON DR SINGH

'I am, as the French say "oeufs sur le plat"'

DEL

'My old man let me down when he walked out and left me to fend for myself. Then my mum died, that weren't her fault but I felt she'd let me down. It's funny the things that go through your head when you're sixteen and all alone. I think that's why I've always been straight and upfront with people'

DEL

DEL: *'Alright, so I might occasionally tell the odd porky or two, but I'll tell ya something I don't do. I don't go around pubs dressed in stockings and suspenders, flashing my boobs at geezers, do I Rodney?'*
RODNEY: *'No, he's never done anything like that'*

RODNEY: *'I ain't laughing. I ain't laughing today, I ain't laughing tomorrow... I don't wanna laugh for the rest of my life'*
ALBERT: *'Well, as long as you're happy, son'*

'I don't believe this! The one job in the paper I really fancied, and it's mine!'

RODNEY

'No, that's stimulated fur, that'

DEL ON RAQUEL'S NEW 'FUR' COAT

'He's been down more holes than Tony Jacklin'

DEL ON ALBERT

ALBERT: *'It's not fair'*
DEL: *'Nor is Frank Bruno's arse but he don't go on about it!'*

'The stars? You don't need to read your horoscope, Rodney, to realise you're in dead lumber'

DEL

'Get up as high as you can Del, eh? You might get a tan'

RODNEY ON DEL GOING HANG-GLIDING

LOVE &
ROMANCE

'I remember me and my missus. I had 18 blissfully happy years... and then I met her'

MIKE

'She is a jealous woman, Rodney. A woman scorned. Now, jealous women are no problem to me normally, you know, I can handle all that, but this one is a jealous woman who's an olive short of a pizza'

DEL

'It's so long since Rodney had a "bit on the side", he didn't know they'd moved it'

DEL

'I think in her own way, she loved me. She never used to charge me as much as the other lads'

ALBERT

'S'il vous plait, s'il vous plait. What an enigma. I get better looking every day. Can't wait for tomorrow'

DEL

'Trying to rekindle the flame in my marriage is like giving a kiss of life to a rasher of bacon'

RODNEY

'In them days, teenage marriages broke up because the husband didn't like The Hollies'

DEL

'Sometimes I think you learnt the art of seduction by watching Wildlife on One'

DEL TO RODNEY

'We are kindred spirits, Janice. Seekers of beauty in an ugly, broken world... Janice... get your bra off'

RODNEY

'I'm 24, Del. By the time you was my age, you'd been engaged to every bird this side of the water'

RODNEY

DEL: *'Well, I've been thinking about her all last night, Rodney. She's had a tough old life. Her old man was a right rough house, all the other blokes she's known before that were no better. You know, she's had nothing but bad luck, then she met me'*
RODNEY: *'Bloody hell, life's a bitch, innit?'*

'It's moments like this that I wish I carried an emergency capsule of Brut around with me'

DEL

'I remember her mum, though. She was a fair sort. Pig ugly but a fair sort. I nicknamed her "Miss 999" you know? 'cause I only phoned her in an emergency'

DEL

'When I approach a bird, she doesn't see the real me; the young, good-looking man about town, own teeth and all that. She sees in her subconscious, a white yacht floating on the blue waters of a Caribbean bay. With you, they see a winkle barge sinking off the end of Southend pier'

DEL TO RODNEY

'Stone me, Del. You've been engaged more times than a switchboard'

RODNEY

'When he was younger, Del's idea of safe
sex was not telling the girl where he lived'

RODNEY

'I can't do all that luvvy duvvy stuff. I feel things
but when I try to say 'em, they always come out...
wallyish'

DEL

'My love life has taken on a distinctly Russian
ambience. Freezing bloody cold and the goods
rarely turn up'

RODNEY

'Grandad, when he said we was going out with a mother and her daughter, I assumed that I'd be with the daughter'

RODNEY

'Rodney can't even give it away, let alone flog it'

DEL ON RODNEY'S LOVE LIFE

'Some of your dates arrive by skateboard'

DEL TO RODNEY

'You've had more dogs than Crufts. The other week, Grandad took your suit to the cleaners. They found a muzzle in the pocket'

DEL TO RODNEY

'There was Monkey Harris draped over a keep left sign, there was Tommy with the handcuffs on, their two wives were fighting like a couple of strays and this plonker was trying to date the arresting officer'

DEL ON RODNEY

'You meet someone you take a fancy to and within a week it's all wine and roses and "I'm just popping down to Bravingtons, Rodney"'

RODNEY TO DEL

'Tonight, in front of half of Peckham, the bird I told everyone was my girlfriend, stood on the counter and took all her clothes off'

RODNEY

'I have just found out that my wife has been lying to me. Every morning she says she's gonna leave me and when I come home, she's still there'

DENZIL

'Say you had got married to her. Can you see what sort of confusion that would've led to? I would've been your father-in-law. Your mother-in-law would've been your aunt, your wife would've been your second cousin. God knows what that would've made grandad; the fairy godmother, I suppose'

DEL

'I have to live with that wedding album for the rest of my life. How many times have you seen a picture of a bride and groom cutting a jam sponge?'

CORRINE

RODNEY: *'I've just met the first girl in my life that really means something to me and it turns out to be my bloody niece!'*
DEL: *'That's why I had to tell you, you see? 'Cause this sort of thing, it ain't allowed. It's... well, it's incense'*

'What a turn-up, eh? He thought he was gonna pull a Swede and she gets lumbered with a cabbage'

DEL ON RODNEY

'I've got so many things worrying me. You know, I mean, the Polar Cap is melting, the continental shelves are shifting, the rain forest is dying, the sea is being poisoned… and I ain't had a bit for months'

RODNEY

'I don't want you lumbering me with some old bow wow who don't know the difference between a Liebfraumilch and a can of Tizer'

DEL

RODNEY: *'I said "don't play with me girl, 'cause you are playing with fire". I said "don't you dare try to tie me down"'*
TRIGGER: *'She's into all that, is she?'*

DEL: *'When she walks in she... well, she lights up a room'*
RODNEY: *'Yeah. Most of your birds walk in and light up a fag'*

'Rodney, you came storming in just at the moment when I was asking Raquel if she would be kind enough to consider stamping my card'

DEL

'The last time you went out with a bird, you took her to a Bay City Rollers concert'

RODNEY TO MICKEY PEARCE

DEL: 'Me and Junie broke up about nineteen and a half years ago, right, that means she was expecting her at the time, which means Debbie is my kid'
TRIGGER: 'But she's a pretty girl'

'Derek, will you get it into your thick skull, I'm not trying to meet intelligent and sensitive people. I'm happy with you'

RAQUEL

'It's alright, Raquel. You don't have to be frightened of the Great Raymondo no more. Del Boy is here'

DEL

ALBERT ON RODNEY'S NEW GIRLFRIEND:
'He told me she looked like Crystal Carrington'
DEL: 'Crystal Carrington? Crystal bleedin'
Palace more like'

'Come on, Marlene. Let's go home and ignore each other for the evening'

BOYCIE

JUNE: 'Debbie won't be a minute.
She's just putting some clothes on'
RODNEY: 'Oh, she needn't bother'

'She was a beautiful woman, a bit like Ginger
Rogers. The last time I saw her, she looked more
like Fred Astaire'

ALBERT ON HIS WIFE

'I started thinking about some of the birds that I
knocked about with and, cor blimey Rodney, some
of 'em have been round the track more times than
a lurcher'

DEL

'Christmas was approaching, Del asked me what I'd like. "Anything you want sweetheart, just name it". So, I said I wouldn't mind a little number by Bruce Oldfield... He got me Tubular Bells'

RAQUEL

'You get on the blower and give Raquel the old S.P. Oh, and tell her to keep on her toes 'cause the last girl I met at Waterloo Station got mugged on the escalator'

DEL

'Girls always blow him out after a couple of weeks. That boy's been blown out more times than a windsock'

DEL ON RODNEY

'You don't know what it's like to have a wife who can't have children. I've tried to console her. I've said "Marlene, God didn't mean you to have kids so shut up about it"'

BOYCIE

RODNEY ON HIS NEW GIRLFRIEND: *'D'you know who she looks like? She looks like that Linda Evans out of Dynasty'*
ALBERT: *'Which one's that, Joan Collins?'*

'I'm fed up having to defend you. The times I've said to 'em "Yes, he's ugly but he's successful"'

MARLENE TO BOYCIE

DEL: *'The old 'uns are the best 'uns, Rodney'*
RODNEY: *'No, we're talking about boats now, Del, not your birds'*

'Linda, nice girl. Had a funny eye. Never knew if she was looking at me or seeing if the bus was coming'

TRIGGER

MONEY

'The government don't give us nothing, so we don't give the government nothing'

DEL

'Come on Rodney, I've told you before. It's everything between you and I, split straight down the middle. 60-40'

DEL

'We've always had something missing from our lives. First we was motherless, then we was fatherless. Now we're flogging one-legged turkeys from a three-wheel van'

RODNEY

DEL: *'Don't worry. This time next year we're gonna be millionaires'*
RODNEY: *'This time last week we were millionaires!'*

'I don't care if it's pesetas, potatoes or Hungarian luncheon vouchers. We're rich!'

DEL

'I'm gonna have to pawn all the jewellery again. Honestly, these rings know more about hock than a German wine taster'

DEL

'Cassandra, we are talking about Derek Trotter. To Del, "Market Penetration" means sex under a barrow!'

RODNEY

'Come on Rodney. This is our big chance. Eh? He who dares wins. This time next year, we could be billionaires'

DEL

'Just think what I could do with a thousand pounds. Fly to America on Concorde, I could buy myself one of those flash Rollox watches...'

DEL

'I remember when you got nicked for riding your motor scooter without a crash hat. You only got fined five quid and you asked for time to pay'

DEL TO RODNEY

DEL: 'But who's to say I won't sell all this tomorrow?'

RAQUEL: 'What are the chances of you bumping into a bald-headed, anti-apartheid, deep-sea-diving Bros fan who has a betamax video recorder, likes Romanian Riesling and whose name is Gary?'

RODNEY: 'I've only got twenty quid on me'

DEL: 'What happened to your wages?'

RODNEY: 'This is my wages'

'He's spent three hours in a stately home and he thinks he's the Earl of Sandwich. You can't wait to get a shotgun and a retriever and go marching across the grouse moors, all done up like a ploughman's lunch, can yer?'

RODNEY ON DEL

'This wonderful land of ours is on the eve of a golden age of the black market... and you and me, we're gonna be in there first'

DEL TO RODNEY

DEL: *'Rodney, I know you may find this hard to believe... and it might even come as a bit of a shock to ya... we are millionaires'*
RODNEY: *'Oh good. Perhaps we can take that magnet off the electricity meter now'*

'We owe two months' rent, we are drinking tea with no milk in it and the Electricity Board keep calling round to see why their meter is running backwards'

RODNEY

'I'm down that casino every night 'til the early hours of the morning, trying to win us some money. If she knew how much I owed 'em, she'd realise how hard I've been trying'

DEL

'In the words of General MacArthur, "I will be back, soon"... I'm not leaving our birthright down there in Davy Smith's locker, no way'

DEL ON DISCOVERING FREDDIE THE FROG'S GOLD WAS BURIED AT SEA

'If Elsie Partridge really could raise the dead then half the money lenders in Peckham would be employing her'

BOYCIE

'A couple of years ago, right, some guru reckoned the world would end within a month and Danny Driscoll bet a grand that it would... and he's the brains of the outfit'

DEL

'I've got so many of his slates under here, I could retile the bloody roof'

MIKE ON DEL

TRAVEL

'I've always wanted to go to Benidorm.
Where is it?'

GRANDAD

'Everything was going well, we were having
a lovely holiday and then they turn up. Within
15 seconds, some sod's shooting at us'

BOYCIE IN FLORIDA

'Rodney, just get me home will yer. Back to
England's green and pleasant land and those
dark, volcanic mills'

DEL

'It's a well-known fact that 90% of all foreign
tourists come from abroad'

DEL

DEL: 'Australia, eh? Where the men are men'
ALBERT: 'And so are the women'

'The British and the Australians are cousins across
the sea. I mean, if your great-grandad hadn't been
a bloody villain, you could've been one of us'

DEL TO AN AUSTRALIAN

'The last holiday we had, the change of climate upset him, didn't it? And we'd only gone to Bognor'

RODNEY ON GRANDAD

'I'm going back to the hotel, to have a fiesta'

GRANDAD

'You look as though you've just come back from a Club 18-30 trip to Chernobyl'

DEL TO RODNEY

'All those romantic places that you've only heard about in fairy tales. The Lee Valley viaduct, the glow of Lower Edmonton at dusk, the excitement of a walkabout in Croydon'

DEL

'Bonjour Trieste!'

DEL

'Rodney, I was up there three hours, three bloody hours! I did loop-the-loop over Dimchurch! There was little kids shouting at me "there goes a spaceman!"'

DEL

ALBERT: 'It's alright Rodney, nothing to worry about. It's just me lungs. We hit a mine coming back from Normandy... I was trapped for twelve hours in a smoke-filled engine room'

RODNEY: 'Well, if it's not one thing, it's another, eh?'

'I wouldn't come home from New Orleans to see Del. I wouldn't come home from the New Forest to see Del'

RODNEY

'You sent me half way around the world. I've been to Amsterdam, I've been to Hull and back!'

DEL TO BOYCIE

'Just get me back to Peckham as soon as possible, otherwise I'll be saying "ay up" and breeding whippets before I'm very much older'

DEL TO RODNEY

RODNEY ON GRANDAD:
'We could take him to Lourdes'
DEL: 'Lourdes! He don't even like cricket'

'That is Bonnet de Douche, as they say in the Basque region'

DEL

MIKE: *"Ere, Del. You speak a bit of French, don't ya?'*

DEL: *'What? Potage bonne femme'*

'Gary!'

RASHID MAHMOON, AKA GARY

LAW & ORDER

DEL: 'Well Boycie, I hope you won't take offence by what I'm about to say but me and Rodney think you've murdered Marlene and buried her in the garden'

BOYCIE: 'How dare you! Murdered my wife and buried her in the garden? I've never been so insulted in all my life. You know how much I've spent on that garden, you think I'm gonna dig a hole in it?'

SLATER: 'I heard a whisper that you're flogging pirate tapes'

BOYCIE: 'Yeah... Treasure Island, Mutiny on the Bounty...'

'I ain't ever been to Rampton. Who started them rumours about me being in Rampton? I ain't ever been to Rampton! I've been to Broadmoor once or twice but that's beside the point'

MENTAL MICKEY

MICKEY PEARCE: 'I had a fight with five blokes last night.'
DEL: 'What was it, a pillow fight?'

'I have a good mind to report your beard to the council'

DEL TO ALBERT

RODNEY: *'Everywhere I went the walls would be whispering "Beast... beast". There'd be posses of 'em waiting for me in the shower room, there'd be razors in my soap, there'd be broken glass in my porridge...'*

GRANDAD: *'Oh, you'd soon learn to adapt, Rodney'*

'I had no choice. If there had been a way of avoiding it, I would have, but his rear light was defective... I mean what else could I do?'

SLATER ON ARRESTING HIS OWN FATHER

'He's got more grasses than Fisons'

DEL ON SLATER

'They seek him here, they seek him there, those policemen seek him everywhere. Is he in heaven? Is he in hell? That damn elusive sha-a-dow'

LENNOX GILBEY AKA THE SHADOW

TRIGGER: 'There's nothing to be nervous about, Denzil. All you've got to do is go in there and tell the truth'

DENZIL: 'Trig, if I go in there and tell the truth, Del and Rodney are going to be spending the next five years sharpening Jeffrey Archer's pencils'

'Oh, they're smashing blokes, Unc. It's like bumping into the Two Ronnies, Biggs and Kray'

RODNEY ON THE DRISCOLL BROTHERS

'It's lucky you're not a judge, Rodney. You'd hang 'em before they finished the oath'

GRANDAD

SPORT

DEL: *'We had Denzil in goal, we had Monkey Harris left-back, we had... we had camaraderie'*
TRIGGER: *'Was that the Italian boy?'*

'I am a black belt in origami'

DEL

'I was a midfield dynamo, me. I used to play like Paul Gascoigne. The one next to me is Boycie; he used to play like Bamber Gascoigne'

DEL

'You can't play draughts on a talking chess game'

DEL

'Kuvera was one of India's premier wicket keepers'

DEL

'Arthur's ashes? That's the black bloke that won
Wimbledon, innit?'

DEL

TRIGGERISMS

RODNEY: *'It's a bit of a mystery all this, innit? It's like something out of one of those Agatha Christie films'*
TRIGGER: *'Yeah, I used to fancy her'*

'If it's a girl, they're calling it "Sigourney" after an actress and if it's a boy, they're naming it '"Rodney" after Dave'

TRIGGER

RODNEY: *'On a cold, rainy night in Peckham, somebody has arranged for you four to be in this room at the same time... and nobody knows who and the most important and frightening aspect of the entire mystery... nobody knows why. Now think hard. Who would do something like that?'*
TRIGGER: *'Jeremy Beadle?'*

'Ain't this coach fitted with a fire distinguisher?'
TRIGGER

'I have to attend lectures on modern climactic change, what with global warming and Al Pacino... you just don't know what's gonna happen next'

TRIGGER

'I don't think you and Del would've won first prize... no. You're alright but Del don't look nothing like Tonto'

TRIGGER TO RODNEY ON HIM AND DEL DRESSED AS BATMAN AND ROBIN

BOYCIE: 'How can you drink with Slater when that's the man who stitched you up over those knocked-off stamps and put you away for eighteen months?!'

TRIGGER: 'I know, but when I come out I got an electric blanket and a radio with 'em'

TRIGGER: 'I sometimes think about the future. I don't want to end up a lonely bachelor like my cousin Ronnie. Then again he did always have a strange taste in women'

DENZIL: 'In what way?'

TRIGGER: 'Well, they were men'

DENZIL: *'That's Derek Trotter in there,
not bloody Einstein!'*
TRIGGER: *'Del knows what he's talking
about and I don't see what the Beatles'
manager's got to do with it, anyway'*

TRIGGER: *'I'm gonna live it up a bit; discos,
nightclubs, golden beaches, blue skies...'*
RODNEY: *'Sounds great, Trig, where are you going?'*
TRIGGER: *'Ireland'*

'I got a room in a motel. They don't know I ain't got a car'

TRIGGER

'I saw one of them old five-pound notes the other day'

TRIGGER AFTER DEL TELLS HIM PEOPLE ARE IMPRESSED BY TALK OF MONEY

'You remember Mike, don't you? He's the water diviner from the Nag's Head'

TRIGGER

No, no not goodbye... no just bonjour

175